NORTH GROSVENORDALE BRANCH

THOMPSON LIBRARY

PURCHASED FROM

THE BEQUEST FUNDS

OF

LEOLYN ELIZABETH MOSHER

PHEBE H. CHANDLER

The Spice Adventure

Julian Messner　New York

The Spice Adventure
by Albert Barker

Illustrated with drawings by the author and photographs

j382
BAR
copy 1G

Copyright © by Albert W. Barker
All rights reserved including the right of reproduction in whole or in part in any form. Published by Julian Messner, a Simon & Schuster Division of Gulf & Western Corporation, Simon & Schuster Building, 1230 Avenue of the Americas, New York, N.Y. 10020.

JULIAN MESSNER and colophon are trademarks of Simon & Schuster, registered in the U.S. Patent and Trademark Office.

Manufactured in the United States of America

Design by Alex D'Amato

Library of Congress Cataloging in Publication Data

Barker, Albert
   The spice adventure.

   Includes index.
   SUMMARY: Describes the great voyages of discovery and exploration undertaken for spices and discusses the history and uses of particular spices and herbs.
   1. Spice trade—History—Juvenile literature. 2. Discoveries (in geography)—Juvenile literature.
   3. Spices—Juvenile literature. [1. Spice trade—History. 2. Discoveries (in geography) 3. Spices]
I. Title.
HD9210.A2B37   382'.41383'09   80-18754
ISBN 0-671-33097-7

*The author wishes to thank the Information Bureau of
the American Spice Trade Association
for information and photographs.*

Messner Books by Albert Barker

The Spice Adventure

From Settlement to City

Black on White and Read All Over

Contents

Introduction 9

CHAPTER 1 Little Brown Sticks 15

2 Spice Merchants of Venice 20

3 The Travels of Marco Polo 23

4 The Voyages of Christopher Columbus 30

5 The Voyages of Vasco da Gama 34

6 Around the World 39

7 The Fabled Spice Islands 43

8 The Dutch Take Over 47

9 Beating the Dutch 49

10 Yankee Enterprise 53

11 True and False Spices 57

12 Spices on the Shelf 60

Spice Dates at a Glance 88

Index 93

Introduction

"Pirates!" shouted the boy excitedly. Perched high above the canvas sails, holding on to the mainmast of the ship, he pointed across the water. "I see their black flag flying."

On the deck the captain handed out arms and ammunition. "Stand by to repel boarders, men." At battle stations the sailors watched a dark shape draw nearer and nearer. They knew these sea robbers were racing to overtake their slow-moving merchant ship. The cargo was very valuable, and the pirates would stop at nothing to get their hands on it. Their cargo? Peppercorns.

In those days, one hundred pounds of peppercorns would bring as much as six thousand dollars—when and if it finally reached London, England.

Fine clothes, silks and satins and jewels were easy enough to buy if you were wealthy. But not even the rich could do anything about the unappetizing food of the day.

There was no good way to keep meats from spoiling or to prepare meats to make them taste good. Then peppercorns were found and made into pepper, then imported around the world. This peculiar black powdery spice could

Weighing peppercorns.

hide the bad odor and taste of decayed cooked meat.

Today pepper costs so little that we never think about it. Yet the spice merchants of Europe used to weigh and count peppercorns as they counted money. Peppercorns were worth their weight in gold. If you had enough peppercorns you could use them to buy land or a house.

Pepper was so expensive because traders, mostly Arabs, ran so many risks to get it. They had to sail the pirate-infested Spice Islands. At any moment these pirates might steal the cargo and the pepper would never reach Calicut in India, the traders' market. Calicut, now known as Kozhikode (koz-uh-kud), was the city where European merchants met the Arab traders and bought their spices. Even if the cargo did get there, a huge pepper tax had to be paid to the ruler of Calicut.

From Calicut the pepper was taken westward across the Arabian Sea and then north across the Red Sea to the city of Suez, in Egypt. Along this route more pirates might

Old drawing of spice caravan meeting ships from Europe.

attack. At Suez, the pepper was transferred to camel caravans for the trip across the desert to Cairo and Alexandria, Egypt. Though the distance was only about 150 miles, progress was very slow, perhaps two miles an hour. Bedouins, a tribe of nomads or wanderers, on their swift horses could easily swoop down and plunder the caravans.

Finally, the spices went on a Mediterranean Sea voyage from Alexandria to the busy Italian port of Venice. At that time the Moslem Turks were in a "Holy War" with the Christians of the Byzantine Empire. Though Venice was often at war with the Byzantine Empire, her principal enemies were the Turks. The Turkish navy often tried to blockade or capture the pepper ships bound for Venice. The Turks won the war, destroying the Byzantine Empire. They forced Venice and the rest of the European states to find some other route to the Spice Islands of the East.

No wonder pepper and other spices cost so much. By the time they were taken north to Europe and England, they were as valuable then as oil is today.

Take a good look at the pepper shaker on the dining table at your next meal. It was the search for a safer, quicker way to transport this spice that sent Columbus, Vasco da Gama, Magellan and others on their historic voyages.

Why did the people in Europe want pepper?
Suppose for a moment you are living in England about 500 years ago. Your parents might be peasants, poor

farmers. Most people were in those days. They did not have last names and most of them could not read and write. There were few schools. You worked with them in the fields from sunrise to sunset, and you were often hungry.

On your way home from the vegetable patch you pick a few onions, turnips and a cabbage to boil into soup and eat with black bread. You and your neighbors have never tasted potatoes, apricots, tomatoes, figs, corn, oranges, lemons, or prunes. Nobody in England has tasted tea, coffee or cocoa. You don't know what sugar is.

So you set down to a flat, dull meal. If there is meat on the table, it probably is spoiled. There is no way to keep it fresh. Your meat has been either salted and packed in a barrel, or pickled in salt water. When it is finally set before you it has a bad odor. It is decayed. You ask your mother, "Isn't there something that we can put on the meat to hide the smell and the rotten taste?" She says she has mixed garlic and onions with it. That's the best she can do.

Across the table your father scowls at his food. "Aye, the rich merchants in London Town and the nobles at Court eat much better. They can afford to pay a few hundred pounds for a spoonful of pepper to conceal the spoiled taste. But we are not rich, Lad."

So you eat the unappetizing food, or you go hungry.

The word "spice" was used to include any root, bark, fruit, gum, sap, leaves, or berries of plants or trees used as flavoring or seasoning.

Spices were also popular with the doctors of the times. The doctors said that cinnamon would cure intestinal pains, and strengthen the heart, stomach and liver. They said almost the same things for cloves and nutmeg. Spices became "miracle drugs," guaranteed to cure anything that ailed you.

The next time you go to the supermarket, stop and look at the spice shelf. Read the labels on the small cans and bottles. It does not seem possible that these easy-to-buy spices were once the causes of wars. Oceans and continents were discovered and explored because of these spices. They were the cause of riches, cruelty, bloodshed, and, as we shall see, spices actually changed the map of the world.

1
Little Brown Sticks

With the blare of trumpets, prayers, and the shout of "God wills it!" a mighty expedition set out for the Holy Land to do battle with the Turks who controlled it. Led by proud barons and knights in shining armor on prancing horses, and followed by peasant soldiers, priests, and thieves, on foot, the First Crusade was leaving Europe to take possession of the holy city of Jerusalem.

Part of this great Christian army marched south through France and the German states, until it came to the city of Venice on the Adriatic Sea. Here the Venetian merchants gave the Crusaders ships and weapons. In return for this help, the leaders of the Crusade promised to trade with Venice after Jerusalem was captured.

The Crusades—nine major and many smaller ones—lasted 177 years. Jerusalem was captured by Crusaders in 1099, but lost in 1187. Except for the first, all the Crusades either failed or were fought to a draw. After each defeat or

long series of battles, the Crusaders straggled home, bringing with them loads of goods. From Persia (the present-day Iran) came cloth called *taffeta,* which means "shine," and cotton *gauze,* a thin fabric named for the Palestinian city of Gaza. Also there was *damask* from Damascus, Syria. A cotton material we know as *calico* came from Calicut. Cotton *madras* came from the city of Madras, India; cotton

gingham from Malaya (now Malaysia); cotton *chintz*, and finally plain cotton, from Egypt or India.

But the most valuable item of all was a load of little brown sticks. What a wonderful aroma they had! When a small piece of the brown spice stick was crushed and mixed with food, it gave the food a delicious taste. The spice? Cinnamon.

Harvesting cinnamon bark in Indonesia.

Cinnamon was used by the Egyptians 2,000 years before the birth of Christ. It was prized by the kings of Egypt, Israel and Persia. Later, wealthy Romans used it in their baths. They also burned cinnamon bark as an incense in their sacred temples.

The Crusaders were curious. Where did this wonderful spice come from? It certainly did not grow in any part of Europe. The merchants of Venice shook their heads. "It comes to us by ship, that is all we know." When Arab traders were asked about this "sweet wood," they answered with fantastic stories, designed to hide the truth:

these little brown sticks came from the bark of trees that grew in a dangerous forest called Paradise. It lay deep in the unknown regions of the Nile River. Nobody dared to go into this enclosure, for Paradise was guarded by flesh-eating dragons, winged serpents, and fierce bats. Once a year these monsters ripped the bark off the Paradise trees. The bark floated down the Nile to secret places where the Egyptians caught it in their nets.

In the year 1096, such a tale was sure to strike terror into the bravest hearts. It kept the Crusaders from searching for the source of the little brown sticks which they liked to put in their cakes, cooked fruits, and other desserts. By scaring the Crusaders away, the crafty traders continued to get high prices for their sweet-smelling, delightful-tasting spice.

But cinnamon did not come from the mysterious forest of Paradise, but from southern and southeastern Asia—what are now the countries of Ceylon (Sri Lanka), Indonesia, and South Vietnam.

2

Spice Merchants of Venice

For hundreds of years the map of Europe and Asia constantly changed as one country conquered another, only to be conquered by yet another country. Wars were fought on land and sea. They were so furious that it became almost impossible to bring spice cargoes from Venice up to northern Europe.

The merchants of Venice were not interested in wars. They were interested in building up their spice trade with Asia. So while northern Europe became a battlefield, Venice became the spice center of the world.

While other European nations struggled through civil wars or border wars, Venice became the world's most prosperous spice seaport. The Italian merchants established trading posts along the Mediterranean seacoast where they could buy spices cheaply. Then they would sell them at fantastic prices to English and French traders who were waiting in Venice.

Among the cargoes of strange spices brought to Venice by the Arab traders was an orange-yellow powder which they called *sa'faran*. This substance was, at the time, in great demand as yellow dye, though it was also being used as a spice. The Arabs demanded a very high price for this unusual spice. They said it was a thousand times more difficult to get than even those precious little brown sticks of cinnamon.

Sa'faran or *saffron,* they explained, came from a brilliant yellow-orange crocus. Each crocus blossom has three stigmas, the sticky ends of the tiny shafts that grow out of the center of a flower. Each stigma holds a tiny bit of the fine powdery dust called *pollen.* The pollen of saffron has to be gathered carefully by hand, a long and tiresome job. It takes 225,000 stigmas to yield just one pound of saffron.

The Venetian merchants had heard so many wild spice stories they thought this was just a trick to make them pay a higher price. But it was one story that happened to be true. Even today, saffron is the world's most expensive spice.

Venice was making great profits from spices. Spain and Portugal were envious. They determined to get their share of the wealth.

Early in the fifteenth century, Portugal's Prince Henry, called Henry the Navigator, was anxious to send ships to explore the African coast to find a way around by sea to India. If such a route could be found, then Portugal would not need Venice to supply her with spices, and, in fact, could take over the spice trade for the whole of Europe.

But before Portugal or Spain could attempt any spice explorations, they had to build bigger and stronger ships. Such ships had to be able to withstand the battering of storms that raged across the unmapped oceans.

Not even Prince Henry knew what lay in the "Sea of Darkness," as the Atlantic Ocean was then known. He did not suspect that another ocean and two immense continents, North and South America, stood between his country and Asia. The prince believed that just across the Atlantic were the lands of Cathay, Cipangu, and the Indies—the Portuguese names for China, Japan and India. But superstitious sailors would not venture westward, no, not for all the spice in the world. They were fearful of stormy winds and lurking sea monsters in the Sea of Darkness. Some of them also believed they would fall off the edge of the world, because they believed the world was flat.

There was a young sailor from Genoa, Italy, who was not afraid of the unknown, and who believed that the world was round. He had read a 200-year-old report by another Italian of the wonderful spices to be found in the Orient, and he believed he could reach them by sea.

The young sailor was Christopher Columbus, a tall, red-haired, blue-eyed mapmaker from Genoa.

The 200-year-old report that Columbus had read was a book called *The Travels of Marco Polo.*

3
The Travels of Marco Polo

Marco Polo was two years old when Nicolo, his father and Maffeo, his uncle, sailed in about 1256 from Venice to the city of Constantinople (now Istanbul), Turkey. The Polos were on a spice and jewel trading trip. They expected to be gone only a few months. But when they were ready to return, too many pirates were roaming the Mediterranean Sea. To return home by land was even more dangerous, for the lonely trails were controlled by bandits.

The Polos decided to travel further east instead, hoping to trade along the way. They reached Russia, but found no jewels or spices. Their caravan continued on across deserts and mountains.

Eventually they came to a great city called Tu-tu, which we now call Peking, in China. They were welcomed by the mighty warlord, Kublai Khan. They became his guests and learned about many oriental spices.

They remained with the Great Khan for many years

and became his close advisors. He would not permit them to leave his court until they promised faithfully to return.

In Italy, their family and friends had long since given up the Polos for dead. They thought Nicolo and Maffeo had died of cold or hunger, or had been robbed and killed by the Moslem Turks, the sworn enemies of Christian Venice.

The return of the Polos in 1269 created a sensation, and so did their treasures from the Orient. There was a peculiar cloth woven from the fur of a shaggy animal called a yak. From the city of Shantung they brought yards of *silk,* spun from the cocoon of worms that ate leaves of a special tree. From Nanking came a yellow cotton cloth called *nankeen.*

Another Polo surprise was a root that had been dug by the Chinese at a place called Gingi in India. We call it *ginger.*

Ginger was used in Greece more than 5,000 years ago to make fancy breads. The Spanish explorers took ginger roots to the Caribbean area after the discovery of the New World. They planted it on the island of Jamaica, and today that is where we get the best of this spice.

The buyers of Polo's ginger roots soon found many uses for them. They added bits of ginger to baked goods, they rubbed it into meats, fowl and fish. They flavored syrup with it.

The Polos also brought home sacks of a spice that

Cultivating ginger in India.

looked like little brown nails. The nails had a delightful perfume and taste. They were really the dried, unopened buds of a small pink flower. The Polos told how the women of Kublai Khan's court always chewed one so that their breath would be sweet when speaking to the emperor.

The Polos asked, but the Chinese would never tell where this wonderful spice came from. It remained a secret for many years, until the Portuguese explorers found the mysterious Spice Islands.

When the French saw the spice, they called them

Marco Polo, from a Venetian mosaic.

clou, which is their word for a nail. In English the word became *clove.*

In 1271, true to their promise, the Polos returned to China and the emperor. This time Marco went with them. He was about seventeen years old and, like many young men, he longed for excitement and adventure. He was also smart enough to keep a record of the far-off places he visited.

Not until the year 1297, when Marco Polo was 43 years old, did he set foot again in Italy. When he did, he found the country at war. Various cities were fighting over boundaries. Venice was trying to overthrow Genoa, and Genoa was attacking Venice. Marco got into the quarrel on the Venetian side. He was captured and imprisoned in Genoa.

While in prison, he met a Frenchman named Rustichello who was a writer. Marco showed him the account of his travels, and Rustichello translated it for him. It is possible, however, that Marco added a few fanciful stories to his real-life adventures. But Marco Polo drew maps that were fairly accurate for the times. His diary was made into a book, *The Travels of Marco Polo,* and it was reprinted many times.

Gathering cloves in the Philippines.

4

The Voyages of Christopher Columbus

There had always been a few scholars who believed the world was round. The trips by the Polo family, and increasingly lengthy sea voyages, caused more and more people to believe this theory. But they could not really understand why, if the world was round, they never fell off.

Columbus knew we wouldn't fall off a round world. And he felt sure that the shortest route to the Spice Islands would be to sail westward across the uncharted ocean.

But Columbus was wrong about the size of the earth. He thought the world was smaller than it really is. If he had known the truth, he might never have attempted the voyage!

To sail westward to the Indies, Columbus needed help—someone powerful to believe as he did. He needed some nation to give him ships and men.

Columbus had served in the Portuguese merchant

marine and learned to draw maps. He had also made several short voyages south along the African coast to buy sugar. It was on these voyages that he first got the idea of sailing westward to reach the East Indies. He decided now to seek the support of King John II of Portugal. In this he was probably encouraged by his brother Bartholomew, who had made at least one long voyage in the service of Portugal.

Portuguese ships were already exploring the African coast to find a route around that continent to the Indies. So King John refused to listen to Columbus. But Christopher was not discouraged. He took his plan to Spain and told their majesties Ferdinand and Isabella what he wanted to do: to sail west and find the Spice Islands of the East Indies. To the king and queen's royal advisors, it sounded like a wild idea.

Ferdinand and Isabella made Columbus wait six years for their decision. He was about to leave Spain and go to France when Isabella approved his plan. And Columbus was ordered to claim any new lands for Spain and to help spread Christianity among the people he would meet. Thus the first great voyage in the world's spice adventure was made possible.

On August 3, 1492, Columbus set sail from the port of Palos, Spain, heading westward with three small caravels and a crew of 90 men. They spent two frightening months, never knowing what lay ahead.

Then, on October 12, 1492, land was sighted—one

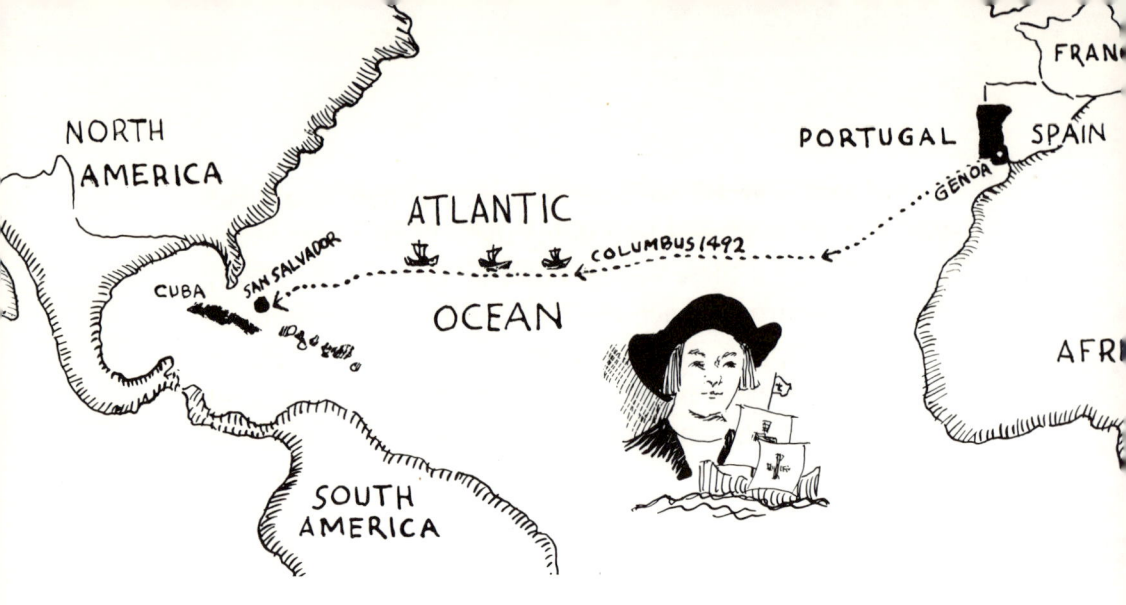

of the Bahama Islands. Columbus named it San Salvador and claimed it for Spain. And then came the big disappointment: there were no golden oriental cities, only miserable palm-covered shacks. In spite of this, Columbus insisted that he had reached the East Indies. He even called the natives Indians.

But where were the spices Marco Polo had described? Where were the silks and gold and jewels? For several months Columbus sailed among what are now called the West Indies, looking for riches. He discovered Cuba and the island of Hispaniola, now the countries of Haiti and Dominican Republic.

The *Santa Maria* was lost in a storm. But Columbus used her timbers to establish a small colony on Hispaniola, leaving 39 men there. On his way back across the Atlantic, Columbus encountered furious hurricanes, and the second ship, the *Pinta*, was lost. But after 224 days out, the *Nina* made it back to Palos.

Columbus brought back a few "Indians," and a cargo of vegetables and tobacco. It was the first time Europeans had ever seen tobacco, pineapples, tomatoes, white and sweet potatoes, corn, sugarcane, or wild turkeys.

But there were no spices.

Isabella, of course, claimed Columbus's discoveries for Spain and immediately made arrangements for more voyages. On his second voyage, 1493-1494, Columbus discovered the island of Jamaica. But somehow he failed to notice the pea-size green berries that grew on tall shiny-leaf evergreen trees all across the island. He didn't wait long enough to watch the natives cut branches from the trees, spread them on the ground and beat them until all the berries came off. The berries were dried in the sun until they turned dark reddish-brown to become the spice we call *allspice*.

5

The Voyages of Vasco da Gama

There is a panic in Lisbon, the capital of Portugal. It is reported that a certain Christopher Columbus, in the service of Spain, has sailed west and reached Asia. Now he has returned. King John II had refused to help Columbus. Now his discoveries would belong to Spain.

Something needed to be done quickly. Portugal's new king, Emanuel the Fortunate, decides to send ships to India before Spain takes over. For this spice adventure, the king needs a courageous leader. In his court is a thirty-seven-year-old nobleman with the reputation of being a daredevil. He is a husky, tough, windburned man who loves the sea. His name is Vasco da Gama.

The king's orders to Vasco are plain: reach India and discover the source of those "grains of paradise," peppercorns. Claim all lands that grow spices of any kind, and

Portugal will become the richest nation in the world.

In 1497, five years after Columbus's first voyage, Vasco da Gama sets sail from Lisbon with four ships. For protection, his sailors paint wide-open eyes on the ships' prows, so the ships can find their way. And the sails carry great red crosses representing the Order of Christ, the Portuguese branch of the famous Templar knights, to which King Emanuel belonged.

Da Gama knew what he had to do, and the very thought was frightening. He had to sail south along the coast of Africa to its tip, around the "Cape of Storms" and into the Indian Ocean.

At the cape, the Portuguese ships ran into storms so furious the sailors want to turn back. Some talk of mutiny, and forget all about spices. Da Gama rallies them. This is not a Cape of Storms, but a Cape of Good Hope, he tells them. When the mutineers refuse to listen he punishes the ringleaders and forces the others to carry on.

All but one of the leaking ships ride out the violent winds and waves, and Admiral Da Gama guides the three remaining ships safely into the Indian Ocean.

When at last Da Gama's fleet dropped anchor in the harbor of Calicut, they had sailed thousands of miles to obtain what we casually pass to each other at the dinner table—pepper.

But Vasco da Gama was not satisfied to reach India. He wanted to locate the actual land where pepper and

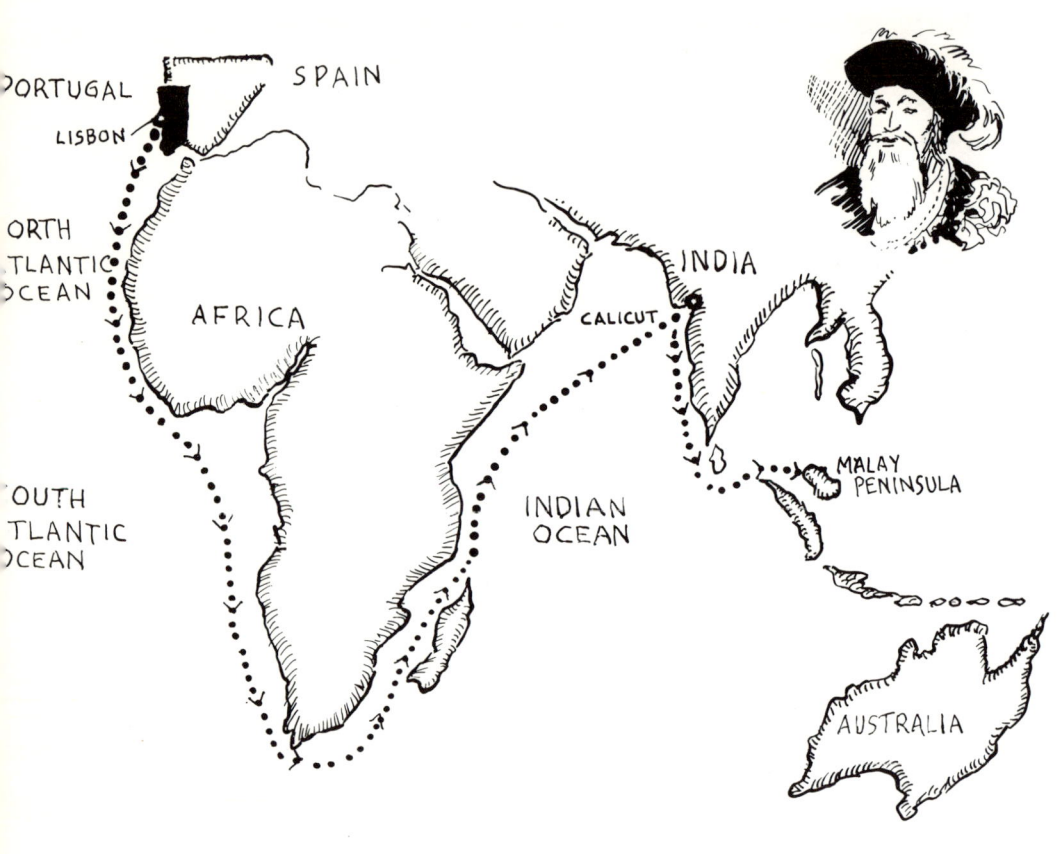

other spices were grown. Then spice ships could sail directly to Portugal. In one master stroke this all-water journey would eliminate Arab traders, Egyptian caravans and Venetian galleys. Portuguese ships would put them out of business.

Ancient spice market in Spice Islands.

In Calicut, da Gama was told about Malacca, a big spice market city on the Malay Peninsula of southeast Asia, far to the east of Calicut. But the Arab traders who controlled Calicut refused to let the Portuguese do business either in Calicut or Malacca. They knew what would happen—the Portuguese would take away the spice business. So da Gama returned home in 1499.

His good friend, Pedro Cabral, was given command of a fleet in 1500 and instructed to get a trade treaty with the rulers of Calicut—or any other country they might visit. But the Arabs tried to sink the Portuguese ships and kill the crews. Cabral had to fight his way into and out of Calicut. Finally, he bombarded the city with his ships' cannons, then left for home.

Da Gama, hearing of this, took a huge fleet of

about 20 ships and blasted his way into Calicut. He returned home with a rich load of spices and other treasures.

In 1503, Portuguese ships finally found Malacca, and in 1511, Affonso de Albuquerque led a fleet against that city, capturing it. By taking Malacca, the Portuguese took control of the entire spice trade. They returned home with another rich load of spices.

But before he had set sail for home, Albuquerque had learned about the secret place of the spices—the place where the Arab traders of Malacca were getting their spices. It was far to the south and east of Malacca, in a group of small islands, some with "fiery hills." Here at last would be the wealth of the Indies.

The Portuguese had heard legends of a place where dried berries, nuts, roots, leaves and spicy bark could be picked up off the ground. In Portugal, these spices would be worth a fortune. The secret place was the Spice Islands, the Moluccas, east of Borneo and west of New Guinea.

King Emanuel lost no time in sending more ships and men to the East Indies, and the fiery, volcanic Spice Islands. Among those who helped take possession of the Spice Islands was a young officer named Ferdinand Magellan. He had been aboard the ships that captured Malacca in 1511. The expedition found such a great wealth of spices that they returned home as fast as possible to get help in conquering the islands.

6

Around the World

In 1519, Ferdinand Magellan was 32 years old. An officer in the Portuguese navy, he had been crippled in a sea battle. But he was a tremendously strong and independent man. It was his blunt way of speaking that annoyed King Emanuel. The king wanted all his subjects to bow down to him and be tame. When Magellan spoke up and asked for higher pay for his services, the king dismissed him, telling him he was free to leave the country.

Magellan went across the border into Spain, leaving Portugal forever. Magellan was certain that he could find a much shorter route by sailing west. Perhaps Spain would be interested.

West? Spain's young King Charles I listened in astonishment. Surely this lame sailor knew about Columbus. He must know that 26 years earlier, Columbus had sailed west and found only miserable shacks, strange natives, and no gold, spices, or riches.

The plain-speaking Ferdinand pointed out on a map

he had made that Columbus could not have found the Indies. "No, Your Majesty, Columbus found new lands. The Indies lie further west, beyond the sea Balboa found. There has to be a passage where a ship can sail through to that sea." Then, Magellan explained, he would sail across that sea and come to the Spice Islands. Magellan did not realize the width of Columbus's land or of Balboa's sea. He figured on a distance of about 600 miles. He found out it was at least 11,000 miles.

King Charles and his royal council considered the Magellan proposal. But Magellan knew their decision would be "yes." Spain was intensely jealous of Portugal, who was fast becoming the top dealer in spices. If Magellan's voyage was a success, Spain could grab a share of the spice treasure.

In 1519, Magellan was given five ships, only to find they were unseaworthy. Their wooden timbers had rotted, their lines and canvas old and worn. To make matters worse, no able-bodied sailors would sign on for the perilous voyage. Desperate to assemble a crew, Magellan went to the jails and hired criminals. He promised them freedom when the ships got back.

After a few hurried repairs, Magellan set sail. During the three-year adventure, four of the five ships were lost in pirate battles, storms, shipwrecks, and mutiny.

In spite of that, Magellan found a strait, a narrow body of water that joined the two oceans so that he could sail from one to the other. The strait was at the southern

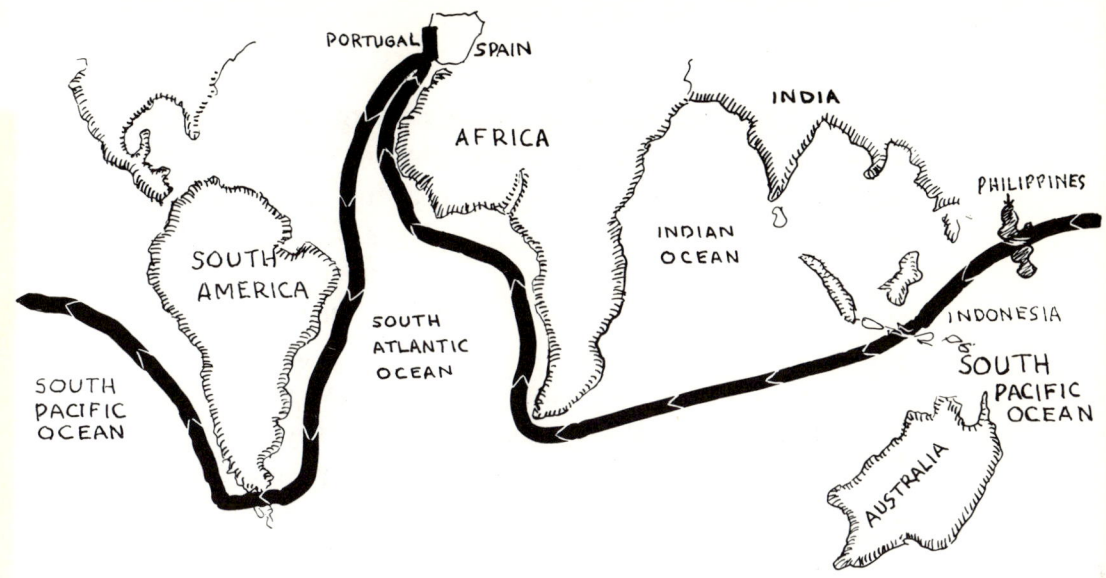

end of South America. It was said that the natives there had never learned how to kindle a flame, so they kept their fires burning all the time. The Spanish sailors called the place *Tierra del Fuego,* Land of Fire.

Sailing through the passage, later named the Straits of Magellan, the ships came at last into Balboa's Great South Sea. Because the water was calm and peaceful, in contrast to the stormy Straits of Magellan, Ferdinand called it *El Pacifico,* the Peaceful Sea. But it was far from a peaceful voyage, for Magellan was killed during a battle with natives in the Philippines.

After Magellan's death, his second-in-command, Sebastian del Cano, completed the voyage. They had sailed west and reached the Spice Islands.

They continued west, across the Indian Ocean to

Africa, following Vasco da Gama's return route. And in 1522, Commander del Cano brought one leaky ship, the *Victoria,* with a crew of 18 worn men into Cadiz harbor. They had gone around the world. Their cargo was a fortune in cloves, cinnamon, mace and nutmeg. It was more than enough to pay for the lost ships and the entire cost of that historic voyage.

Commander del Cano had bad news also for the Spanish monarch. Portuguese ships were already in the South Pacific and had taken Malacca. They were gaining possession of the Spice Islands, too. The king immediately outfitted a fleet of ships, ordering them to go south and fight Portugal's claims.

For seven years there was a bitter quarrel. But in 1529, King Charles decided the search for spices was not worth the fight. The Spanish king had learned of a fantastic fortune in gold to be taken from the South American Incas in Peru. He thought this was more attractive than spices. Charles sold his rights to the Spice Islands to his brother-in-law, King John III of Portugal, for 350,000 ducats (about $812,000). And Portugal was left in command of the spice trade—for the time being, at least.

7

The Fabled Spice Islands

As the Portuguese sailed among the Spice Islands, they had a terrifying experience. One dark night the men were awakened by a violent rocking of the ship and a rumble like thunder. They rushed on deck and watched in terror as flames from beyond the forest shot up into the sky. A few minutes later, the flames died away, and red-hot ashes began to fall on the water and on the decks. A volcano had erupted.

Next morning the island looked peaceful in the brilliant sunlight, but the frightened crew quickly up-anchored and left. They passed among many volcanic islands where networks of rivers wound back into dense forests and rich valleys. Fortunately, they did not know that they were also in the most dangerous earthquake belt in the world.

Yet these were the most sought-after islands in the world—the Moluccas. They lie in a curving trail that arches out eastward from the larger East Indies islands of Sumatra, Java and Borneo. The Moluccas are not far from Australia to the south. The name "Molucca" was first used in 1609, and is said to have come from an Arabic word *malak,* meaning a "king." Each of the larger Spice Islands had its own king. To get cargoes of spices, the Portuguese had to deal separately with each king.

Gathering spices was difficult. Among the spice trees were snakes, scorpions, and crocodiles. There was a constant fight against ants, flies, and millions of tiny bugs. At night, mosquitoes tormented the men. Then, too, the kings demanded merchandise, not money, in exchange for spices. Merchandise was hard to land and they didn't want to bother.

Secretly, the Portuguese made plans to bring in a company of soldiers to get rid of the kings and take the Spice Islands for Portugal.

Meanwhile, they continued to trade. One of the Portuguese's favorite spices was nutmeg. The nutmeg aroma was so powerful that often the islands' birds grew dizzy from smelling it. The nutmeg trees grew as high as 70 feet. Their fruit looked like an apricot. To gather the fruit, the natives used long poles with prongs and a basket attached. The prongs loosened the fruit which fell into the basket. When ripe, the fruit split open and showed a dark brown nut inside. And it produced a bonus, a second spice, called mace. Mace is the bright red lacy covering of the nut, and inside the nut is a seed of nutmeg. Mace has a sharper

Nutmeg fruits before they ripen.

flavor than the sweet, delicate nutmeg seed.

Our great-great grandmothers often wore small silver nutmeg graters on their necklaces to scrape a bit of the spice into their tea.

After the mace and nutmeg were left to dry for a few days, they were ready for shipment. Into the Portuguese ships also went peppercorns and a spice called *cardamom*. Cardamom is the dried pepperlike seed of the ginger family. It has become one of the world's most popular spices.

The Portuguese controlled most of the East Indies and the spice market for over a hundred years. By about 1580, they were so rich and powerful they thought they would never lose their hold on the spice trade.

Separating mace from nutmegs, Indonesia.

But it was in 1580 that Portugal lost its independence to Spain. It became little more than a Spanish province for the next 60 years. During this time, Spain's chief enemy was the Netherlands. The Spanish managed to control parts of that country for over a hundred years. And because of the bitter warfare going on between the Dutch and the Spanish, anything the Spanish owned was in danger of attack from the Dutch. It was this war against Spain that cost Portugal all of its Spice Islands and its trade.

8

The Dutch Take Over

Before Spain conquered Portugal, the Portuguese king had expanded the spice trade by going directly to merchants in France and England. To do this, more ships were needed. Instead of building them, the king looked around for vessels and crews for hire. He found them in the Netherlands.

The Dutch were good sailors as well as shipbuilders, and they had an expanding merchant marine, eager for trade. So the Portuguese hired a Dutch fleet to bring spices from Lisbon up along the coast. At each French and English port, Portuguese officials took charge of the precious cargoes, selling them to the highest bidders.

After Portugal lost its independence to Spain, a Dutch captain named Cornelius Houtman got hold of a secret map showing the sea routes to the South Pacific. He took it to the Dutch merchants in Amsterdam. "Why should the Spanish make all this spice money?" he asked. "Are we not as good sailors and businessmen? Why not get into the spice trade, too?"

Dutch merchants and political leaders were interested in any plan that would hurt the Spanish, with whom they were fighting a bitter war.

And so they formed the Dutch East India Company in March 1602, sending an armed fleet to the East Indies. Their invasion of the former Portuguese possessions started a furious island-to-island war. The Dutch made friends with the native kings, and helped them get rid of the hated Portuguese. In return, the kings gave the Dutch exclusive rights to their islands' spices.

By 1610, Spain had been driven from all but one island. The Netherlands took over the Malay Peninsula, Sumatra, Java, and the Spice Islands. Now the Dutch were the undisputed masters of the East Indies, which were now called the Dutch East Indies, and the spice trade.

The Dutch turned out to be more ruthless than the Portuguese and Spanish were. Natives who sold spices to anyone but the Dutch were quickly executed. The Dutch deliberately destroyed thousands of spice trees to make the spice scarce. If the price of cinnamon fell too low in Amsterdam, they burned the spice in the islands. Or they soaked the nutmeg in lime water. This did not affect its flavor but was supposed to make it impossible for the nutmeg to be planted. Then, because of the resulting shortage, the Dutch were able to ask higher prices.

9
Beating the Dutch

It was hard for the Dutch to protect every one of the Spice Islands. Other nations resented the Dutch monopoly. A Frenchman named Pierre Poivre (whose name in English would be Peter Pepper) soon discovered there were some fifty or more islands that were not guarded. He decided to send an expedition to a few of these islands and take them over for France. He was sure that spices could be grown in France's new tropical possessions, especially on the islands of Mauritius in the Indian Ocean.

In 1770, Poivre and his men "kidnapped" more than 400 nutmeg and 70 clove trees, as well as 10,000 nutmegs and a chest of cloves, some of which had sprouted. Two years later an even greater quantity was taken. The plants were distributed among other French islands, especially that group of islands off the coast of Africa known as the Seychelles. All the plants flourished.

The people on the great secret spice plantations of

Transporting pepper, India.

the Seychelles burned their clove trees in 1780. Pirates flying the British flag appeared in the harbor. The French did not want their enemies to get their precious spices, so they destroyed them. It turned out that the pirates were French after all. But the clove trees were gone just the same.

The British ended the Dutch spice trade as well.

For many years the British had been looking for a sea route to the riches of the East. In 1527, a British merchant, Robert Thorne, suggested to Henry VIII that a

search be made for the "northwest passage" across North America to India and the Indies. The Spanish held the westward route by way of the Straits of Magellan. The Portuguese held the eastward route around the Cape of Good Hope. "It is for us to discover a northwest passage," declared Thorne.

The British made many voyages in search of the northwest passage. These led to important discoveries in North America, but they did not find the passage to the rich land of the spices. The British then began to eye the rich spice trade of the Dutch East Indies.

In 1600, the British East India Company was chartered by Queen Elizabeth I. Thousands of her subjects were sent into southeast Asia. Beginning in 1623, disputes with the Dutch turned to violence. The Dutch murdered all the members of one British spice trading post. This stopped the active expansion of the British East India Company in the Dutch Spice Islands.

The Dutch were stubborn fighters. The British fought three fierce wars with them between 1652 and 1678, mostly over matters of trade. Neither side won a clear victory, but the Dutch navy finally weakened and allowed the British to get the upper hand.

By 1780, the British held Malacca and almost all the Dutch islands and trading posts. To top it off, the Dutch East India Company was caught in a financial scandal, and almost went bankrupt. It was finally dissolved in 1798.

By the nineteenth century, Great Britain was "Mistress of the Seas," and led the world in the import of spices.

The British imagined the spice trade would never again change hands. But then came a surprise from a least expected part of the world.

In North America, the thirteen colonies south of Canada were already getting into the spice business without the permission of the mother country.

10

Yankee Enterprise

King George III of Great Britain wanted those "Yankees" out of the Spice Islands. But the Yankee sea captains of New England paid little attention to him. They knew that Britain had her hands full trying to handle the French, and meanwhile they could make millions of dollars by bringing pepper directly to the colonies.

The Yankees remembered Elihu Yale, and how he worked for the British in Madras, India, from 1670 to 1692, making a fortune in spices. He used his spice money to help a small college at Saybrook, Connecticut. With his money this college moved to New Haven and, in his honor, changed its name to Yale College (later Yale University).

When the American colonists won their independence, one of the first American spice merchants was a Yankee sea captain named Jonathan Carnes. Carnes sailed his clipper ship, *Cadet,* to southeast Asia in 1788. On the island of Sumatra he discovered a surprising source of

peppercorns. No Europeans had discovered these valuable vines before because they grew in the mountainous interior. The Dutch and English never ventured in there, and for a very good reason. Fierce Malay tribes lived in the hills and they killed anyone who entered their territory.

Captain Carnes was willing to take the risk. He and most of his men raided the Malay trees, and the *Cadet* returned home safely, after a two-year voyage of twenty-four thousand miles. His cargo in Salem, Massachusetts, harbor caused a sensation.

When news of the *Cadet*'s voyage reached other New England ports, shipowners organized fleets to do as Carnes did. Between 1795 and 1873, about one thousand ships made the long and dangerous voyage, bringing back millions of pounds of spices.

Through the seventeenth, eighteenth and early nineteenth centuries, all spice ships had to be on the lookout for pirates. American spice ships often heard the warning cry of "Pirates!" shouted from the lookout's perch to the clipper deck. Pirates, or buccaneers, as they were also called, would wait in hidden harbors along the Atlantic coast. They would dash out and board heavily-laden homeward-bound ships and steal the cargoes.

Many ships were taken this way. The crews were killed or sold into slavery, and the stolen cargoes sold. Pirates became so bold that the United States government sent ships to attack pirate bases on land to stop the plundering. In fact, the United States fought the Tripolitan War

against pirates of the Barbary Coast of North Africa. The war lasted 15 years, until the United States finally won in 1815.

With the pirates out of the way, Salem's pepper trade flourished. The spices were sold in apothecary shops (what we now call drugstores) to be used for medicines, and in the homes of the well-to-do.

But the voyages to the South Pacific for spices slowly died out as the United States found it more profitable to trade for spices with other countries.

11
True and False Spices

The United States imported all kinds of new seasonings, including dried leaves and seeds. These leaves and seeds were not true spices—such as cloves, cinnamon, nutmeg, pepper—but they were called "herbs." They included leafy herbs such as chervil, basil, sage, and marjoram. And seeds of caraway, mustard, sesame and poppy

Fields of basil being cultivated in California.

were sometimes called herbs.

Today more than 180 spice plants are known. An interesting herb, growing in popularity today, was introduced to Europe by the Polos. Called *jen-shen,* it was a rare herb that grew wild. Anyone who could find it was said to be granted eternal life. Today, *ginseng* is specially grown, and we can find it in special shops in this country. Ginseng is used by some people as a medicine and tonic.

Is something like *vanilla* a spice or an herb? Thomas Jefferson may have asked that question, too. When he was in Paris with John Adams in the 1780s, they were served some sweet-flavored cakes. Jefferson asked what spice was in them, and was told, "vanilla." Jefferson's host made him a present of 200 chocolate-brown

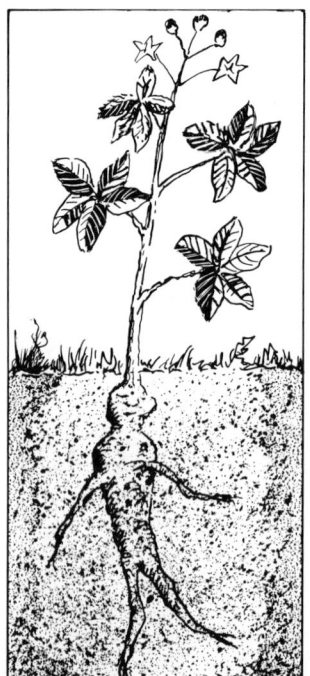

Ginseng Root

"vanilla beans." He said they were from a climbing orchid. The beans are dried for a year. Then the flavor is extracted, or taken out, by cooking the beans in a large vat with alcohol. The result is vanilla extract, something you can probably find in your own kitchen. Today vanilla is known mainly as a flavoring, but it would be more accurate to call it a spice, since it is used to improve the taste of food.

Thomas Jefferson may have been surprised to learn that the vanilla beans he got in France came originally from just across the border from the United States: Mexico. The vanilla orchid had been cultivated there since the time of the Aztecs. Hernando Cortes, the Spanish conqueror of Mexico, had tasted it in chocolate drinks in the palace of Montezuma.

12

Spices on the Shelf

Because the United States has every kind of climate, from tropical heat to arctic cold, from fertile soil to desert sand, many spices and herbs that once grew in other lands are now grown here. Some can even be grown in your own home.

The United States has become the most important spice importer and consumer in the world. New York City is the center of the American spice trade. About three million pounds of spices, herbs and aromatic seeds are brought into this country each year. Another million pounds are grown here, particularly in California. Domestic products include red peppers, cayenne peppers, paprika, basil, tarragon, mint, parsley, sage, marjoram, and seeds such as mustard, dill, fennel, and sesame.

After they are carefully inspected by the U.S. Food and Drug Administration, the spices are sent to grinding plants. Here they are again inspected before being processed in various types of mills and packaged.

In the early days, cloves, cinnamon, pepper, nutmeg and other spices were bought whole, for spices retain their flavor much better when they are not cracked or ground. You can still buy spices whole, but most of the time we buy them already ground.

The following is a list of those spices and herbs you can find on the shelf in your neighborhood grocery store. The word "grocery" itself comes from the time when English pepper merchants were known as *grosserii,* a French word for measurement when weighing spices.

ALLSPICE

When the Spanish arrived in the Caribbean area, they found large parts of the island of Jamaica covered with strange trees bearing aromatic berries. When dried and tasted they seemed to combine the flavors of nutmeg, cinnamon and cloves. The Spanish called this fragrant spice *pimenta,* or pepper, but it has no relation to peppers. It is really a member of the myrtle family.

Allspice berries, whole or ground, are now used to

season pot roast, mincemeat, and plum pudding. It is delicious, too, with cakes, pies, tomatoes, and sweet yellow vegetables. Allspice reaches us from Jamaica, Honduras, Guatemala, and Mexico.

ANISE (AN-is)

The Romans considered these small gray-brown seeds to be magical. They were used as a charm to prevent bad dreams, to cure snakebite, and after a banquet to cure indigestion. Anise seed tastes like licorice, but licorice comes from a root. It is used for seasoning all meats, for chicken, duck, and in cookies, cakes, fruit, and compotes. Anise was first found in ancient Greece and Egypt. We now import it from Spain, Turkey, and Syria.

BASIL (BAZ-ul). Also called SWEET BASIL

Basil means "royal." The ancient Greeks gave basil its name. This delightful smelling leaf of the mint family is a native of India and Iran. It was once planted around temples and homes to insure happiness. The basil is very popular in Italy. Many a young Italian wears a sprig of basil as a sign of being in love.

Basil leaves are bright green, and when dried are used to spice pizza, tomato dishes and spaghetti sauce. The leaves add an appetizing aroma to vegetable soups, peas, green beans, and cucumbers. A few fresh leaves can be chopped and used for flavoring salads. Basil is now grown in the United States, but is also imported from France, Hungary, and Belgium. You can grow fresh basil in a garden and even in a window pot. A few fresh leaves can be chopped up and used for flavoring salads.

BAY LEAVES

There are many legends connected with bay leaves. Daphne, a beautiful nymph (a spirit or minor goddess) in Greek legend, was fleeing from the god Apollo. To help her escape, the earth goddess Gaea (JEE-uh) turned her into a sweet bay or laurel tree.

Bay leaves have become a symbol of victory and honor. Our word *baccalaureate,* the degree you get upon college graduation, comes from the laurel tree and its berries, and to win laurels meant a wreath of bay leaves given as a prize.

The tree is a native of the Mediterranean Sea area. Its leaves are large, measuring up to three inches in length. Their aroma is unusual and has a strong flavor. One or two dried bay leaves is enough for a pot of stew or soup. Most bay leaves are imported from Turkey, Portugal, Greece, and Yugoslavia.

CAPERS

The caper bush still grows wild on the mountain slopes near the Mediterranean Sea. In the Middle Ages capers were taken as medicine to prevent disease. Capers are neither a fruit nor a seed. They are really unopened flower buds. Today the best capers come from the south of France. They are gathered and salted or soaked in vinegar and bottled. Capers are often used when making sauces, or with vegetables like eggplants, and are very good in potato salad.

CARDAMOM SEED (CAR-duh-mum)

The Vikings discovered cardamom in their travels a thousand years ago. This is why it has been widely used in Scandinavian dishes for many centuries. Many Danish pastries carry the slightly camphor-like aroma of these tiny seeds. Cardamom is also sometimes called cardamon. It is a native of India and grows wild there on mountainsides. The seeds are used in making curry powder. They also give a fine flavor to baked goods, apple and pumpkin pies, and you can taste them in certain kinds of sausages.

Several varieties of cardamom comes mainly from Sri Lanka, India, and Guatemala. The smaller seeds are good for barbecuing, for basting sauces and for pickles.

CARAWAY SEED

Because the caraway seeds are easily broken, they are harvested at night or while they are still covered with dew in the early morning.

Roman soldiers brought the seed from Asia and spread them throughout most of Europe as they conquered one country after another.

This plant belongs to the parsley family and grows best in the Netherlands. Most of the caraway seed we use comes from that country. We also import some from Denmark, Poland, the Soviet Union and Syria. The seed is sold whole and is easy to use. You find it in rye bread, in cheese, scattered over pork and sauerkraut dishes, soups, meats, and stews. They should be crushed before using to release their flavor.

CAYENNE PEPPER

Cayenne peppers, sweet peppers, pimentos, and chili peppers are the fruits of various plants belonging to the family known as *capsicum*. They are America's main contribution to the world of spices, for they are all native to this continent.

When the Spanish arrived in the New World, they found a variety of pepper plants bearing pods of several shapes and sizes. The Indians of Mexico called them chili. Some of them were mild, but others were called "devil" peppers and the taste seemed to burn the tongue.

Cayenne peppers, hottest of all the spices, is used in making pizzas and other Italian dishes, and is put in tabasco sauce. This sauce is named for a river in Mexico. Cayenne, sometimes called red pepper, is not related to the ordinary black and white pepper you find on the dining table.

CELERY SEED

Celery seed is the fruit of wild celery. In many countries the plant is grown for use as a medicine. It takes more than 750,000 of the tiny brown seeds to weigh a pound. You can buy them whole or as celery salt, which is a mixture of the ground seeds and table salt. Either one is excellent with fish, in soups, tomato juice, potato salad, eggs and many other foods.

The crunchy celery stalks you eat are not the same as the celery seed plant. There is a distinct difference in flavor. Celery is grown in the United States and celery seed is imported from India and France.

CHILI POWDER

During World War II, it was not easy to get Asian or European spices. So Americans learned to use more chili powder. This is a blend of spices: chili pepper, ground cumin seed, ground oregano, powdered garlic, and salt. It is a very hot spice. Chili powder is used to season shellfish, hard-boiled and scrambled eggs, gravy, hamburgers, and chili con carne.

CINNAMON

Cinnamon was once the most distinguished and most expensive of the spices. It was the most difficult of all spices to transport to Europe. Cinnamon also has the oldest history. Cinnamon wood and cassia, which is another form of cinnamon, were highly valued in ancient Egypt. It is said that Cleopatra carried it with her jewels. Cinnamon made from cassia is not as good as true cinnamon. But it is popular in China, and is known as Chinese cinnamon.

The bark of cinnamon wood, which is thin and brittle, is a pale yellowish brown on the outer surface and a darker brown inside.

Cinnamon is the dried bark of a certain kind of evergreen tree. The tops of these trees are cut off. This forces small branches to grow from the trunks. The natives cut these branches and carefully peel off the bark. The hot tropical sun soon dries and curls the bark. Then they are put inside a larger stick of curled bark to make what is called a "quill." The cinnamon quills are rolled into mats which are tied together to form a large bale for shipment.

Oil of cinnamon is distilled from the bark and is used in the treatment of stomach disorders. At one time cinnamon was mixed with other aromatic substances and made into a paste. It was pressed into the shape of a small ball and carried as a protection against colds and other infections.

Today cinnamon is one of our most important baking spices. When ground into a powder we use it in stews, in buns, breads, cookies, and cakes. You can taste it in many chocolate desserts and drinks. Cinnamon is no longer rare, but it still tastes wonderful.

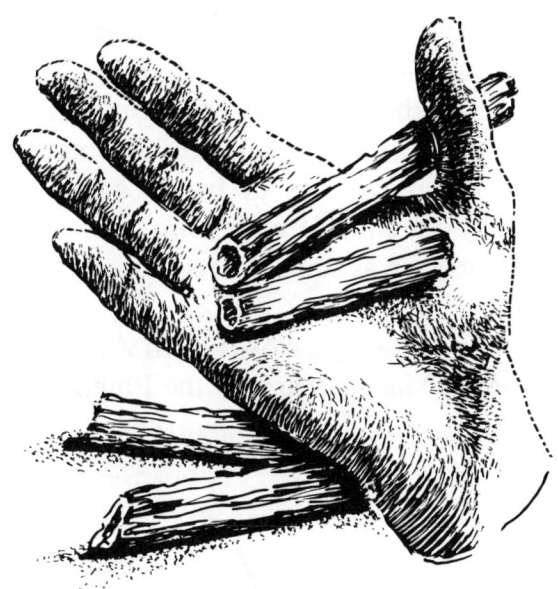

CLOVES

The clove tree is one of the most beautiful of all tropical evergreens. It grows to a height of from 12 to 20 feet. Its leaves hold tiny oil glands, and on still, hot nights the scent of a grove of clove trees can be detected from a great distance. Although clove buds were eagerly bought in Europe to add flavor and fragrance to food, they were never used in any way by the island natives.

It takes from 4,000 to 7,000 dried clove buds to make a pound. Clove stems have been used to dye silk, and oil of cloves was given to relieve stomach aches. Clove oil is also used in the perfumery and cosmetics industry. Because it has such a clean taste, it is often found in toothpaste.

We use cloves in baked goods and in desserts, especially in chocolate mixtures. Cloves improve sweet vegetables such as squash, beets, sweet potatoes, and boiled onions.

Today we get cloves from Zanzibar (now a part of Tanzania), Madagascar and the Philippines.

CORIANDER (koh-rih-AN-dur)

When green, the coriander plant and seedpod have an unpleasant smell. But when dried, the pods drop off and the seeds have an agreeable odor. In ancient times, magicians burned coriander to make incense which, so we are told, would conjure up an army of devils.

The coriander seeds have been found in Egyptian tombs. The Old Testament tells of *manna,* the food eaten by the Israelites during their wanderings in the desert, and describes it as being like coriander seeds. Some people call the plant Chinese parsley.

Today coriander is used to hide the unpleasant taste of medicines. It flavors candies, apple pie, gingerbread, and hot dogs.

It is imported from Morocco, Argentina, Rumania, and France.

CUMIN SEED

Cumin seed is an important ingredient in chili powder and curry powder because of its strong taste. The seeds look like tiny ears of corn. They smell and taste a lot like caraway seeds.

Many superstitions have clung to cumin seed: that it is the symbol of the miser: that a happy life awaits a bride and groom who carry cumin seed during the wedding ceremony.

You'll find this tiny seed in chili con carne, pork

and sauerkraut, and in some cheese made by the Swiss and the Dutch. We import it from Morocco, Lebanon, and Syria.

DILL

"Dill" comes from the Norse word *dilla,* meaning "to lull." Norse mothers thought that an extract of dill seeds, when given to babies, would lull them to sleep.

In earlier times, dill was used by doctors as a medicine. The Greeks thought it had magical powers. They believed that holding a dill plant in the left hand could prevent nervous diseases. Another myth was that dill would help you to sleep soundly, and that it would cure hiccups.

We use the seed in the production of dill pickles and in dill vinegar. Dill is grown in the United States, but much of it is imported from India.

FENNEL SEED

In ancient times, some people believed that fennel was one of the sacred herb-spices that could prevent nine different diseases.

Marathon is the name of an ancient Greek town where a great battle took place, and messengers ran 26 miles to the city of Athens to carry the news of the victory. But few people know that *marathon* is also the Greek word for fennel. The Battle of Marathon was fought on a field of fennel plants.

Someone wrote in 1657, that seeds, leaves and roots of fennel would cause people to lose weight. There was also a story that when a fennel plant was stuck in the keyhole of a bedroom, the sleepers would not be disturbed by evil spirits.

Today we simply use the seeds to add a good taste to apple pie, cakes, and cookies. We get fennel from India and Argentina.

GINGER

In Roman times emperors often used ginger instead of pepper. The Chinese grew the ginger plant in pots aboard their ships as a source of fresh green food, as a protection from diseases on long sea voyages. In the 1500s, Queen Elizabeth I liked to have fancy cakes baked with ginger and served to her guests. Ginger was once called "the richman's spice" because it often cost as much as pepper.

Ginger mixed with honey was sold as a cough medicine.

Ginger comes from a reedlike plant that is native to Asia. The ancient Greeks imported it from merchants in western Asia.

Only the root is used. We can buy it whole, cracked or broken into small pieces, or ground into powder. You have tasted this favorite spice in gingersnaps, ginger ale and in baked goods.

Ginger is imported from Jamaica, India, and the African countries of Sierra Leone and Nigeria.

MACE. *See* **NUTMEG.**

MARJORAM (MAHR-joh-rum)

The name comes from the Greek and means "joy of the mountains." The Greeks planted it on graves to signify peace and happiness for the departed. As a medicine it was once used to rub on sprains and bruises.

Marjoram belongs to the mint family. The leaves are gray-green in color and they have a sweet smell. When dried they have many delightful uses. They flavor lima beans, green beans, and peas. They add to the flavor of lamb, mutton, and poultry. Marjoram is mixed with other spices in making liverwurst, bologna and headcheese.

Most of the our marjoram is brought in from France, Portugal, Greece, and Rumania. It is also grown in the United States.

MINT

There are many members of the mint family. An old saying about mint, "If you want to count all the names of mint, you have to be able to say how many fishes swim in the Red Sea."

However, while members of the mint family include basil, rosemary, marjoram, sage, and oregano or sweet marjoram, none of these are true mint plants—they are just related. The true mints are spearmint, peppermint, and pennyroyal.

According to Greek mythology, *Minthe,* sweetheart of Pluto, the god of death and the underworld, was changed into the plant which still bears her name. The smell of mint was supposed to stimulate the appetite.

Peppermint is one of the most used flavorings for candies, gum, perfumes, and for soaps. Spearmint is important as a food and gum flavoring, too. Its spear-shaped flower spikes are sweet, with a cool aftertaste.

Mint is sold today as flakes or leaves. It is a very popular flavor for frozen desserts, for chocolate, and many fruits. Mint can be cooked with peas and carrots. Mint jelly or mint sauce are often served with roast lamb.

Mint is grown all along the west coast of the United States. It is also imported from Belgium, France and West Germany.

MUSTARD

A book could be written about the superstitions and legends woven around mustard. It is the name for a very large family of plants.

The Chinese have cultivated various kinds of mustard since ancient times. The name comes from Latin *mustus,* which means "fresh" or "new." *Mustus* was new wine (that is, wine freshly made), which was the chief ingredient in the paste that we now call mustard.

A legend dating from 1664, states that mustard is

supposed to "quicken and revive the spirits, strengthen the memory, and expel heaviness."

A mustard plaster, or paste of mustard on a cloth, was applied to the chest or back to cure headaches, fever, cough, asthma, or stomach complaints. Some singers mix mustard with honey to cure a hoarse voice.

Millions of people like mustard, for today it takes more than 400 million pounds to satisfy the annual world demand. Mustard is used to add taste to meats, fish, fowl, salad dressings, cheese, and dishes made with eggs. This spice is different from all other spices. It has no aroma as long as it remains dry. But when mixed with water or wine, its full flavor develops.

Two principal types of mustard plants are grown: white and black. The seeds of these two plants are very similar. The mustard paste we use on hot dogs is made from ground mustard flour, mixed with other spices and herbs.

Mustard seed is grown in this country, and we also import it from Canada, Denmark, and Great Britain.

NUTMEG and MACE

The beautiful nutmeg tree is the only one that gives us two spices instead of one. The fruit is apricot in color, and about two inches across. When ripe, it splits open so you can see the lacy crimson covering of the nut, mace. Inside the nut is a seed. This seed is the nutmeg. Nations once eagerly sought, bought and fought for nutmegs.

Mace is used to flavor pound cakes, cherry pies, and fish sauces. Whole nutmegs are often grated into foods, which adds to their flavor. These include baked goods, puddings, sauces, vegetables, and drinks. Nutmeg is used in chicken soup, in candied sweet potatoes, and eggnog.

Today it grows not only in the Moluccas, but in other tropical countries, and in southern Florida.

PAPRIKA (puh-PREE-kuh)

Paprika is the Hungarian word for red pepper. But Hungarian red pepper is mild. Originally grown in Hungary and throughout central Europe, paprika is now grown in California, too.

Paprika contains lots of vitamin A and C. The Hungarian-American scientist, Dr. Albert Szent-Gyorgyi (shent-jee-AWR-jee), helped discover vitamin C. He found out a lot of facts about this vitamin by extracting it from paprika. For his work on vitamin C, he was awarded the Nobel Prize for 1937.

Most of the paprika sold in the United States is the sweet type. It is called a "garnish spice," used for an attractive appearance. You will see paprika on salads, fish, meat, and chicken, in soups, egg dishes, and vegetables. You can taste it in hot dogs and in catsup.

Unfortunately, some paprika on the market is a fake, and has less taste than chalk dust. The best American paprika is the sweet type, grown in California. It is also imported from Spain, Yugoslavia, Morocco, Bulgaria, and of course, Hungary.

PEPPER

The king of all spices. Pepper has been the "master spice" all down the centuries. Here is a verse from *Alice in Wonderland:*

> I speak severely to my boy,
>   I beat him when he sneezes:
> For he can thoroughly enjoy
>   The pepper when he pleases.

In addition to hiding the bad taste of meat, pepper was also supposed to make you sneeze and thus clean the brain. The word comes from the Latin *piper* (pronounce pipper), which means pepper, too. Black and white pepper are taken from the same plant—a climbing vine. In the early days of the spice trade, pepper was imported in bunches just as it grew.

Black pepper is made from the red berries picked before they are fully ripe. They turn black and shrivel up in the sun. These are the peppercorns. White pepper is made from the ripe berries. They are prepared by soaking them in water, then rubbing off the softened outer skin. White pepper has a milder taste than the black.

POPPY SEED

At least 400 different kinds of plants have the name poppy. Poppy seeds come mostly from the corn poppy. It takes about 900,000 poppy seeds to weigh a pound. These tiny blue seeds are so small that one pod in a plant may hold 30,000. Like so many of our spice seeds and herbs, poppies were originally grown near the Mediterranean seacoast. In India they are roasted with honey to make a dessert.

Each poppy seed holds a tiny droplet of oil, which has a sweet nutlike flavor. The oil is used in artists' paints and as a fine salad oil. The seeds are sold in whole form, to feed birds, and for cooking and spices. You will see them sprinkled on rolls, breads, cookies, and pastries.

They can also be crushed and mixed with sweetenings as a filling for pastries. When mixed with melted butter, poppy seed makes a delicious dressing for green beans, potatoes, fish, noodles, or rice. Poppy seed is imported from Denmark, the Netherlands, Sweden, Balkan countries, Turkey, and Argentina.

ROSEMARY

The plant gets its name from the Latin *ros maris,* which means "spray of the sea." Many legends have grown up around this plant. One tells how, during their flight into

Egypt, the Virgin Mary rested by a bush of rosemary, over which she threw her shawl. Then, as if by magic, the white flowers turned a heavenly blue in her honor.

Ancient people often used rosemary in their religious ceremonies. It was used at one time to beautify the hair, to prevent baldness, and cure headaches.

Rosemary leaves look like inch-long pine needles. They are very good as a spice for lamb, chicken, eggplant, turnips, cauliflower, green beans, other green vegetables, and in marinades. The leaf has a strong flavor and must be used sparingly.

Rosemary now grows in California, but we also import it from France, Spain, Yugoslavia, and Portugal.

SAFFRON

The saffron plant has been known in Egypt and southern Asia for thousands of years. In ancient India, saffron was cultivated for its yellow dye which was used to color veils and religious garments. Saffron is now too expensive for dyeing purposes. It was mentioned in Biblical times and Crusaders may have known about it. It was brought to Spain by the Arabs, and from there it spread to the rest of Europe and to the New World. The American saffron and meadow saffron are, however, not the saffron we use as a spice. Today we get most of our saffron from Spain and Portugal.

Saffron is used to add taste and color to rolls and chicken and rice dishes.

A tiny pinch of saffron will instantly color anything it touches. When saffron first reached England, the nobles mixed it with their tea to give it a rich golden color. They said it was like drinking gold. They also found that saffron could be used to give a fine golden-brown color to their leather saddles and harness.

SAGE

Sage was once regarded as a miracle plant, and has long been used as a seasoning for food and medicine. The leaves were supposed to strengthen the memory. Perhaps this is why a wise man is often called a sage. Slender and green when picked, sage leaves turn silver-gray when dried. It is a member of the mint family.

For many years sage has been used in the United States. It has a strong fragrant odor, and you smell it when used as a seasoning and stuffing for turkey, or in baked fish, salad dressing and chowder. Sage comes in whole, rubbed, or ground form.

The principal users of sage are meat-packers and sausage makers. The plant is cultivated in many lands, but most of it comes from Yugoslavia, and other areas of southern Europe.

SESAME SEED (SES-uh-mee)

These small pearly white seeds are one of the world's oldest spices. They have been used as a food in the Middle East, Africa, and the Orient for many centuries. Greek and Roman soldiers carried sesame seeds as food when going on long marches. The seeds have a rich, nutlike flavor when baked on rolls, buns, and bread. Sesame seed is always sold whole.

Some of these seeds come from Texas and California. We also import sesame seed from Mexico, Guatemala, and El Salvador.

TARRAGON

The name comes from the Greek word for "dragon." This is because its roots have a serpent-like shape. It is a native of Siberia. Few people knew about tarragon until the thirteenth century. Years ago, Spanish doctors declared that it would sweeten the breath, put you to sleep, and hide the taste of bitter medicine.

The slender, pointed leaves have a very slight licorice taste. In the grocery store you can get tarragon vinegar and sometimes tarragon salad dressing. It is a seasoning for chicken and seafood and egg salad.

Tarragon is grown in the United States and imported from Yugoslavia and France. It is sold in the whole form.

THYME (pronounce TIME)

Thyme was a symbol of sweetness, courage and elegance to the ancient Greeks. The Romans thought a person would stop being sad or unhappy if he or she stuffed the pillows with thyme.

The gray-green leaves of thyme belong to the mint family. It has been a favorite in American kitchens for many years. It goes into clam chowder, poultry stuffing, and it flavors cottage cheese. Oil of thyme is used in some cough drops. You can buy thyme in whole or ground form.

We import it from Spain, France, and Portugal, but some is grown in the United States.

TURMERIC (TUR-mer-ick)

Turmeric is a plant of the ginger family. The roots have a strong yellow color and are valuable when used to dye cloth. In many eastern countries women use turmeric and water to give their skin a golden glow.

Turmeric is one of the main spices in curry powder. Today it is sold in ground form for use in all kinds of everyday dishes. It is very good in chicken, seafood, with rice, creamed potatoes, and macaroni. It is imported from India, Jamaica, Peru, and Haiti.

Spice Dates at a Glance

50,000 B.C. By this time archeologists believe humans had noticed that certain leaves impart a delicious flavor to meat.

2300 B.C. In one of the earliest written records, Assyrians tell of their gods drinking sesame seed wine before they created the earth.

1920 B.C. Biblical history tells of Joseph (of the coat-of-many-colors) being sold to a spice caravan by his brothers.

1520 B.C. The Book of Exodus in the Bible tells of Children of Israel fleeing Egypt, taking with them "principal spices."

1453 B.C. Greeks began the Olympic Games at which victors were awarded laurel (bay leaf) wreaths.

902 B.C. Queen of Sheba visits Solomon with "camels that bear spices" as her principal gift.

80 B.C. Alexandria, Egypt becomes the greatest spice trading port of the eastern Mediterranean, with one of its entrances known as "Pepper Gate."

50 B.C. Romans bring mustard seed to England.

65 A.D. Funeral rites for Nero's wife Poppaea in Rome consumes an entire year's supply of precious cinnamon.

900 A.D. Venice rising as a commercial power—much of it based on spices—beginning to bring Europe out of the "Dark Ages."

1179 Guild of pepperers founded in London; Pepperers to become Guild of Grossers in the fourteenth century.

1298 Marco Polo returns from China; tells where spices grow and awakens western world's interest in trading directly with the Orient.

1418 Portuguese Prince Henry the Navigator establishes his navigation college to spur worldwide spice quest.

1492	Columbus sails to seek a more direct passage to the Orient's spice riches, opening Age of Discovery and Exploration.
1498	Vasco da Gama reaches Calicut, India, the spice center.
1505	Portuguese discover Ceylon (the present Sri Lanka), an important source of cinnamon.
1511	Portuguese capture Malacca, very important spice center; they also discover the Spice Islands.
1519	Magellan sails westward in the service of Spain, looking for new spice lands; a lone surviving ship returns, with enough spices to finance a new expedition.
1529	Charles I of Spain (also known as Charles V of the Holy Roman Empire) cedes to Portugal all the rights that Spain had claimed in the Spice Islands for 350,000 ducats ($812,000).
1585	West Indies ship arrives in Europe with first cargo of Jamaica ginger—first oriental spice to be grown successfully in the New World.

1599	Dutch establish first trading posts, in the Banda Islands, and on Amboina and Ternate, all part of the Spice Islands group (Moluccas).
1600	British East India Company founded.
1602	Dutch East India Company founded.
1640	Dutch seize Malacca and control of most of spice production in the East.
1760	Large amount of cloves and nutmeg burned at Amsterdam to keep the prices up.
1770	Pierre Poivre of Mauritius steals cloves and nutmeg seeds from Dutch and starts new growing areas on his island, thus affecting the first breech in the Dutch East Indies monopoly.
1797	Captain Jonathan Carnes of Salem, Massachusetts returns from Sumatra (Dutch East Indies) with first large cargo of pepper and puts the United States into world spice trading.
1805	The United States reaches the peak of its Sumatra pepper trade; re-exports alone totaled seven million pounds in one year.

1873   Piracy and native hostility finally snuff out direct American pepper trade with Sumatra, and the last of the 967 pepper voyages is completed.

1937   Professor Szent-Gyorgyi wins Nobel Prize for his research with vitamin C, which he got mostly from the spice paprika.

1940   First commercial paprika crop grown in California.

1969   Spices reach the moon, as seasoning in astronauts' food.

1970   The per capita spice usage in the United States reaches an all-time high of 28.8 ounces annually, up 56 percent since 1960.

1971   Spice trading with China re-opened as the United States ends 21 years' embargo on trade.

Index

A
Adams, John, 58
Albuquerque, Alfonso de, 38
Allspice, 33, 61
America, spice merchants, 53
Amsterdam, 47
Anise, 62
Apothecary, 56
Arabian Sea, 11
Arabs, 10, 12, 20-21, 37, 83
Atlantic Ocean, 22
Australia, 44
Aztecs, 59

B
Bahama Islands. *See* San Salvador
Balboa, 40
Barbary Coast, 56
Bartholomew of Portugal, 31
Basil, 57, 60, 62-63
Bay leaves, 63-64
Borneo, 44
British, 50-53
Byzantine Empire, 12

C
Cabral, Pedro, 37
Cadet, (ship), 53, 55
Calico, 16
Calicut, India, 11
California, 60
Cano, Sebastian del, 41
Capers, 64
Cape of Good Hope, 35, 51
Capsicum. *See* Pepper
Caraway seed, 58, 65
Caravels, 31
Cardamom, 45, 65
Caribbean, 61
Carnes, Jonathan, 53
Cassia. *See* Cinnamon
Cayenne pepper, 66
Celery seed, 67
Ceylon/Sri Lanka, 19
Charles, King of Spain, 39
Chervil, 57
Chili powder, 67
China/Chinese, 22-23, 27, 73, 76
Chintz, 17
Chocolate, 59
Cinnamon, 14, 18-19, 42, 8, 57, 61, 68-69
Columbus, Christopher, 12, 22, 30-33, 34, 39-40
Constantinople/Istanbul, 23
Coriander, 71
Cortes, Hernando, 59
Crusades, 15-19, 83
Cuba, 32
Cumin seed, 71

D
Damask, 16

Dill seed, 60, 72
Doctors, 14
Dominican Republic, 32
Dutch East India Company, 48, 52
Dutch. *See* Netherlands

E
East Indian Company, 52
Egypt/Egyptians, 11, 12, 18-19, 71, 83
Elizabeth I, Queen of England, 52, 73
Emanual, King of Portugal, 34, 38
England/English, 9
Europe, 20
Exploration, 21, 22

F
Fennel seed, 60, 72-73
France/French, 27-28

G
Gauze, 16
Ginger, 25, 73-74
Gingham, 17
Gold, 42
Great Britain (England), 52, 77
Great South Sea, 41
Greece, 25, 62, 63, 72, 73, 75, 76, 85, 86
Grocery, origin of word, 61

H
Henry VIII, King of England, 50, 64
Henry the Navigator, 21
Herbs, 57, 60

Holland. *See* Netherlands
Holy Land. *See* Crusades
Houtman, Cornelius, 47
Hungary, 79

I
Incas (Peru), 42
India/Indies, 11, 30, 83
Indian Ocean, 41
Indonesia, 19
Iran. *See* Persia
Italy/Italians, 22, 25

J
Jamaica, 25, 61
Japan/Cipangu, 22
Java, 44
Jefferson, Thomas, 58-59
Jerusalem, 15
John, King of Portugal, 31

K
Kublai Khan, 23, 26

M
Mace, 42, 44. *See also* Nutmeg
Madagascar, 70
Madras, India, 16, 53
Magellan, Ferdinand, 12, 38-41. Straits of, 51
Malacca/Malaya, 17, 37-38, 55
Manna. *See* Coriander
Maps, 20, 36, 41
Marathon, battle, 72-73
Marjoram, 57, 60, 75
Mauritius, 49
Meat, 13-14
Mediterranean, 20, 23
Mexico, 59, 66

Mint, 60, 75
Montezuma, 59
Moluccas, 44, 52
Mustard, 58
Mutiny, 35, 40

N
Netherlands, 46-50, 65
New England, 53
New Haven, 53
New York City, 60
Nile River, 19
Nina, 32
North America, 52
Northwest Passage, 51
Nutmeg, 14, 42, 44, 48, 49, 57, 61. *See also* Mace

P
Pacific Ocean, 41
Paprika, 60, 79
Paradise, 19
Paris, France, 58
Parsley, 60
Pepper, 9, 35, 53, 57, 60, 61, 80-81
Peppercorns, 9, 10, 34, 45, 55
Persia/Iran, 16, 18
Philippines, 41, 70
Pimento. *See* Pepper
Pinta, 32
Pirates, 9, 23, 40, 50, 55, 56
Pizza, 66
Poivre, Pierre, 49
Pollen, how gathered, 21
Polo, Marco, 22-23, 25-30
Poppy seed, 58, 81-82
Portugal/Portugese, 21-22, 34, 38, 42, 45, 46

Prince Henry of Portugal, 21-22

R
Red Sea, 11
Romans, 62, 65, 73, 85, 86
Rosemary, 82-83
Russia, 23
Rustichello, French writer, 29

S
Saffron, 21, 83-84
Sailors, 22
Sage, 57, 60, 84-85
Salem, Massachusetts, 55-56
San Salvador, 32
Santa Maria, 32
Sea of Darkness, 22
Seseme seed, 58, 85
Seychelles, 49-50
Ships, 37-38, 40, 42, 47. *See also* named ships
Silk, 25
South America, 41
Spain/Spanish, 31, 33, 39, 61, 66
Spice, 14, 17, 21-22, 25, 30, 44, 60, 61
Spice Dates, 88-92
Spice Islands, 11, 12, 27, 30, 31, 38, 42-43, 53
Spice merchants, 10, 36
Sumatra, 45, 53
Supermarket, 14
Syria, 16
Szent-Gyorgi, Alfred, 79

T
Taffeta, 16
Tarragon, 60, 86
Templar Knights, 35

Thorn, Robert, 50
Thyme, 86-87
Tierra del Fuego, 41
Trading posts, 20
Turks, 12, 15-16
Tumeric, 87

U
United States, 55, 57, 60
U.S. Food and Drug Administration, 60

V
Vanilla, 58-59
Vasco de Gama, 12, 35
Venice, 15, 18, 20-21
Victoria (ship), 42
Vietnam, South, 19

Vikings, 65
Virgin Mary, 83
Volcanos, 43

W
War, Dutch/English, 52
Dutch/Spanish, 46
Island-to-Island, 48
Tripolitan, 55
Venice/Genoa, 28

Y
Yak, 25
Yale College, 53
Yale, Elihu, 53

Z
Zanzibar (Tanzania), 70

3 4038

copy 1G

j382   Barker, Albert
Ba
           The spice adventure

DATE DUE

THOMPSON LIBRARY